KT-552-849

INTRODUCTION

Construction machines can be found wherever any building work is being done, from putting up small houses to laying long roads. Over the years, these mighty machines have replaced the work of hundreds of people. Today, enormous shovels can gouge huge holes in the ground, boring machines can dig long tunnels deep underground, and excavators can pull down tall buildings.

Front bucket
The front of the bucket is
hinged so that the rubble
can be easily dropped into
a waiting truck. The bucket
on this backhoe loader can
lift nearly 3 tonnes of rock.

Engine power
The engine provides all the
power to drive the backhoe
loader, including raising the
front bucket with a load of
rubble and moving the
backhoe to dig.

Chunky tyres
The backhoe loader
has large, chunky
tyres to drive over
rough ground.

FIFE COUNCIL LIBRARIES

FC359469

LOOK INSIDE MACHINES

DIGGERS

JON RICHARDS

Franklin Watts
London • Sydney

© Aladdin Books Ltd 1999
New edition published in 2003

Designed and
produced by
Aladdin Books Ltd
28 Percy Street
London W1T 2BZ

First published in
Great Britain in 1999 by
Franklin Watts
96 Leonard Street
London EC2A 4XD

ISBN 0 7496 5090 7

A catalogue record
for this book is available from
the British Library.

Printed in UAE

Editor
Michael Flaherty

Consultant
Steve Allman

Design
David West
Children's Book Design

Designer
Simon Morse

Illustrators
Simon Tegg & Ross Watton

Picture Research
Brooks Krikler Research

Jon Richards has written a
number of books for children
on a wide range of subjects.

CONTENTS

Backhoe

At full stretch, the backhoe can reach out, or down, as far as the combined height of three adults. It is moved by controls at the back of the driver's cab.

BACKHOE LOADER

This unusual-looking machine is possibly the most useful digger on any building site. It has tools fitted to its front and to its back. On the front is a huge scoop, or bucket, which can be used to scoop up rubble. On the back is a movable arm, called the backhoe. This can be used to dig trenches or pull down buildings. It can also be fitted with different tools to do other jobs, such as a pneumatic drill (*see* page 18) and a mechanical claw.

Stabilisers

These special arms reach out to take the weight off the back wheels and provide a steady platform when the backhoe is being used.

Diggers can come in

Foundation piles

When a tall building is being put up, it needs very deep foundations to stop it from sinking into the ground. Special cranes fitted with huge drill bits (*below*) dig holes into which the foundation piles are sunk.

Dredger

Not all diggers are used on land. A dredger (*above*) digs up mud from the bottom of the sea or a river. This stops the waterway from getting blocked.

all shapes and sizes.

Skid steer

This tiny building machine (*below*) is called a skid steer. It is very useful in small spaces because it can turn very tight corners.

Mini excavator

A mini excavator (*left*) is used where space is tight. With its small arm and bucket, it can dig very narrow trenches. The body of the excavator above the tracks can rotate in a full circle.

Engine
The engines used to power excavators need to be very strong. They can be nearly four times more powerful than the engine used to run a family car!

Cab
The cab is fitted with large glass screens to give the driver a good view of the excavator's arm.

In a spin
The top half of the excavator can spin around in a full circle. This lets the excavator dig up rubble from one side and drop it into a truck on the other side, without moving anywhere.

Caterpillar tracks
Caterpillar tracks have ridges to stop vehicles from slipping on soft or icy ground.

Hydraulic arm

The engine pumps fluids in and out of hydraulic rams on the excavator's arm. Inside these rams, the fluids push pistons in and out, moving the arm.

Hinged bucket

The bucket on an excavator is hinged, allowing it to be moved up and down, like your wrist.

Sharp teeth

As the arm pulls the bucket back, sharp teeth on the front of the bucket cut through the rubble and earth, scooping them up into the bucket.

EXCAVATOR

These mighty machines are seen on the largest building sites. They are used to dig the foundations beneath buildings, or to dig wide trenches. Their strong hydraulic arms (*see left*) are also used to pull down buildings, or they can be fitted with enormous claws to pick up heavy objects. Beneath the driver's cab are two large Caterpillar tracks. These spread the weight of the excavator over a larger area and stop it from sinking into soft ground. The largest excavators can weigh 80 tonnes – that's as much as 25 fully-grown elephants!

There are many ways

Going, going, gone

Not all buildings can be demolished cheaply and quickly by machines. Very tall buildings may need dynamite to knock them down. Sticks of dynamite are put in places in the building where they will have most effect. When they explode, they cause the building to collapse (*right*). It takes a lot of skill to demolish a building without damaging surrounding buildings and spreading rubble everywhere!

to knock things down.

Bulldozer

When a building has been knocked down, the rubble has to be cleared away. Machines called bulldozers (*below*) are fitted with huge blades at the front. They push the debris to one side where it can be loaded into trucks.

Giant claw

The claw on the end of this machine (*right*) is used to pull down buildings. The driver's cab is fitted with bullet-proof glass to protect the operator.

Machines are used to

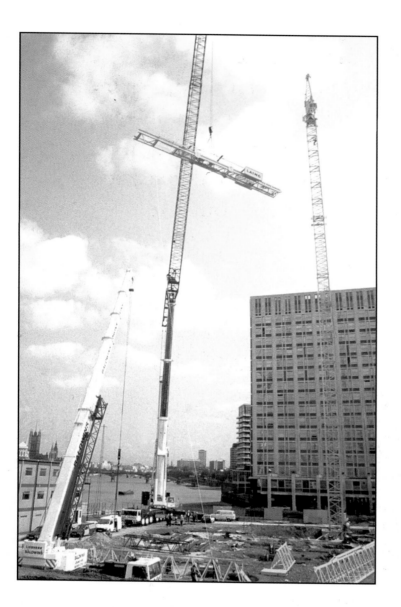

Tall cranes

The tallest cranes are put together in stages (*left*). They have long arms, or jibs, which sit on top of towers. Loads are lifted by cables and a hook from one end of the jib, while heavy weights on the other end stop the crane from falling over. This is called a tower crane.

Eye in the sky

The crane driver sits in a small cab at the top of the crane (*right*). From here, he or she controls where the crane's arm is pointing and how much cable is run out to lift or lower the load.

lift things into the air.

Into the air

Once they have been set up, cranes are used to lift almost any object into place. It could be a section of pipe (*left*), metal girder, some glass for a window or a load of concrete.

Movable cranes

Not all cranes have to stay in one place. This mobile crane (*above* and *right*) is fitted on a special truck. It has a long arm which can be extended and spun around.

Pick and shovel

Today, a single machine operated by one person can do the same work which used to take many people equipped with picks and shovels (*right*).

Full steam ahead

Before powerful internal combustion engines and electric motors were invented, building machines were powered by other means. This shovel (*above*) was powered by a steam engine.

building much easier.

Trench digging

Endless bucket trenchers use a series of small buckets on a belt. As this belt moves around, the buckets scoop out the earth to dig a trench. Bucket trenchers, like this one from 1901 (*right*), were used for many years, long before the invention of hydraulic arms (*see* page 9).

Steam press

Like the steam shovel (*see far left*), this roller (*left*) was powered by a steam engine. The roller's huge, heavy wheels were used to squash the surface of a road flat to make it smooth for vehicles to drive over.

Rear engine

This scraper is fitted with two engines. The engine at the rear drives the rear wheels, pushing the scraper along.

Collecting the load

This container can hold about 17 tonnes of earth – that's nearly the weight of 250 adults!

The blade

The scraper's blade can be pushed up to 30 cm (12 in) into the soil.

SCRAPER

This machine is used to scrape up layers of earth, preparing the ground for a road. It has a huge blade underneath which digs up

Hinged front

The tractor unit is linked to the rest of the scraper by a large hinge which bends to make turning easier.

Tractor unit

The front of the scraper, which contains one engine and the driver's cab, is called the tractor unit.

Powerful engines

In order to push and pull the scraper's blade through the ground, the engines need to be very powerful. Each engine on this scraper is as powerful as the engines from ten family cars!

he soil as the scraper drives forward. The soil is then collected n a huge container and carried o another site where the scraper can drop it. Sometimes, even the two engines on a scraper are not powerful enough and it may need to be pushed by another vehicle.

Digging it up

This backhoe loader has been fitted with a pneumatic drill (*left*). In this, air is squashed very hard, which forces a piston up and down. This piston smashes onto a tool, hammering it into the road.

Fine grades

A grader is fitted with an angled blade. As the grader drives along, this blade pushes the soil to one side to create the flat and even surface. This is called grading. It can also be used to create even slopes (*below*).

used to build a road.

Squashing it flat

After the asphalt has been laid (*see* pages 20-21), a roller (*left*) is used to squash it flat and make it smooth. The heaviest roller can weigh 35 tonnes – that's the same as 12 elephants!

Excavator

As well as demolishing buildings and digging trenches, excavators can be used to build roads (*left*). Their buckets can be used to move rubble and to grade soil to create an even surface.

Exhaust

As the engine burns fuel to work, it creates waste gases. These gases are carried out of the engine along a metal pipe called the exhaust.

Controls

On some road pavers, the steering wheel and other controls can be moved from one side of the paver to the other. This lets the driver keep a close eye on either side of the road.

Hopper

Tipper trucks empty the hot asphalt into this large hopper at the front of the road paver.

Conveyor belt

This conveyor belt carries the asphalt from the hopper to the rear of the road paver.

Hotplates

Once the asphalt has been spread over the road, special heated plates, called soleplates, flatten and smooth the asphalt out. Sometimes, these soleplates can be extended so that the paver can lay a wider road.

Giant corkscrew

At the back of the road paver is a large screw called the auger. This auger spins slowly, spreading the asphalt evenly across the road.

ROAD PAVER

Once a pathway has been dug for a road, the road's foundations are built by putting down layers of materials. The final layer is built by a road paver. This noisy, smelly machine moves forward slowly, spreading a thin layer of asphalt. This is a black, sticky substance which is mixed with stones. It can be squashed and shaped when it is hot, and is rolled flat by a roller (*see* page 19) to make it smooth. When it cools, it sets hard enough to withstand heavy traffic. A paver is also used to replace old or damaged asphalt.

Massive machines

Wheel and bucket

This enormous machine (*below*) is used in huge opencast mines. It is fitted with a massive wheel which is ringed with buckets. It is called a bucket-wheel excavator. The huge wheel at the front of the excavator spins around and the buckets gouge out earth.

Life's a drag

This massive digging machine (*left*) is called a drag-line excavator. It throws out an enormous bucket on the end of a cable and then drags it back over the surface. As it is dragged back, sharp teeth on the front of the bucket scrape up the earth.

Massive buckets

The buckets on a mining excavator need to be big (*right*). The largest buckets are wide enough to hold two family cars!

Strong arm

The hydraulic arm of a mining shovel has to be strong enough to lift the bucket and a full load of rock. In some cases this load can weigh as much as five adult elephants!

Bucket

The tip of the bucket has sharp, strong teeth to break up the rock. The bottom of the bucket is hinged so that the mining shovel can drop its load.

MINING SHOVEL

Not all mines are hidden deep beneath the ground. Sometimes, minerals lie close to o on the surface. To get at these minerals,

Night lights
On top of the cab are powerful headlights which allow the shovel driver to work even after it has gone dark.

Swing gear
Underneath the driver's cab is the machinery which spins the mining shovel around in a complete circle.

Twin engines
Inside many mining shovels are two powerful engines, creating as much power as 35 family cars. The shovel can still operate even if one of the engines breaks down.

huge machines (*see* pages 22-23) dig up the rock, creating enormous mines called opencast mines. One of these machines is a mining shovel. When it has filled its bucket, the driver can spin the shovel around and drop the load into a waiting truck.

Machines are used to

Long tunnel

The world's longest rail tunnel is the Seikan rail tunnel in Japan. It is 54 km (33.5 miles) long. It runs under the sea between the main island of Honshu and the island of Hokkaido. Here (*right*) you can see some of the machines used to dig the tunnel.

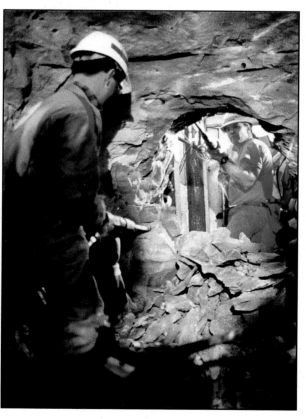

Under the sea

The Channel Tunnel runs between England and France. Tunnel-boring machines (*see* pages 28-29) took over four years to dig the tunnel. This picture (*left*) shows the exciting moment when the two halves of the tunnel were linked.

tunnel underground.

Cutting coal

In an early underground coal mine, people had to dig the coal out with picks and shovels. Today, machines are used to cut coal from the coal face – the exposed coal on the walls of the mine (*above*).

Exploding walls

This machine (*left*) is used to drill lots of little holes into a mine wall or coal face. The holes are loaded with explosives which are then set off. The wall shatters and falls to the floor. The rubble is gathered and removed.

Cutting head
The cutting head is fitted with 100 cutting rollers and 200 picking teeth. These are made from a very tough metal called tungsten.

Conveyor belt
This belt carries the rubble away from the tunnel face to waiting trucks.

Drive motor
This huge electric motor spins the cutting head. The cutting head rotates about 1.5 to 3 times every minute.

Push and pull
This motor makes sure that the cutting head is in the right position to cut the rock efficiently.

TUNNEL-BORING MACHINE
Creeping forward at a speed of 12 cm (5 in) a minute, these long machines are

Fixing the segments
The segments lock together snugly and the joints are filled. In some cases, the tunnel may need to be watertight, so segments are bolted together and rubber seals used.

Concrete segments
The tunnel is lined with concrete and iron segments, each weighing up to eight tonnes!

Carrying the segments
Each segment is lifted from its train wagon by a special crane. This crane then lifts the segments onto a special trolley which carries them along the tunnel.

used to dig tunnels. These tunnels can run under the seabed, through a mountain or beneath busy city streets. At the front of a tunnel-boring machine (TBM) there is a huge cutting head that can rotate at different speeds to cut away the rock.

Fantastic facts

• The largest mining excavator ever built is a dragline excavator called Big Muskie. It weighs 12,000 tonnes and has a bucket capacity of 168,000 litres (37,000 gallons)!

• The Italian inventor and artist Leonardo da Vinci designed the first rotating crane in 1480.

• The pneumatic drill was invented in 1861 by the French engineer Germain Sommeiller. It was first used to build the Mont Cenis Tunnel which runs under the Alps.

• The tallest mobile crane in the world is the Rosenkranz K10001. It weighs nearly 900 tonnes, but it can lift nearly 1,120 tonnes. Its arm can reach a height of 202 m (663 ft).

• Caterpillar tracks were invented in 1904 by American inventor Benjamin Holt. They were first used on a tractor in 1908.

• The tunnel-boring machines used to dig the Channel Tunnel were 15 m (49 ft) long and weighed 1,300 tonnes. Behind them were trains, each some 180 m (590 ft) long and with over 1,000 tonnes of equipment.

Building words

Backhoe
The extendible hydraulic arm at the rear of a backhoe loader. It digs by using an inward movement.

Caterpillar tracks
These are wide belts which are fixed to a vehicle instead of wheels. They spread the weight of the vehicle over a large area and stop it from sinking into soft ground.

Hydraulic
This refers to objects which are moved or powered by a liquid, such as water or oil. Hydraulic rams are used to move the arms in most diggers.

Internal combustion engine
An engine where the burning of air and fuel occurs inside the engine's cylinders. Steam engines are not internal combustion engines because their fuel is burnt outside the engine.

Piston
A rod which fits inside a cylinder and is moved up and down by the pressure of a gas or a liquid.

Pneumatic
This refers to objects which are moved or powered by compressed air, such as a pneumatic drill.

Index

PHOTO CREDITS

Abbreviations: t-top, m-middle, b-bottom, r-right, l-left, c-centre.
Pages 5, 9 & 19m – Charles de Vere. 6 & 18t – Roger Vlitos.
6-7, 11m, 12t & 13 all – Liebherr UK Ltd. 7m – JCB. 7b,
11b & 18b – Courtesy Finning UK Ltd. 10 all, 12b, 16,
19b, 23b, 26, 26-27 & 28 – Frank Spooner Pictures. 14
both & 15 – Mary Evans Picture Library. 21 – Blaw
Knox. 23t & 27t – Eye Ubiquitous. 24 – Eric
Blackadder. 27b – National Coal Board.